KEY VOCABULARY FOR U.S. HISTORY

John Marshall Carter

ISBN: 978-1-312-10868-1

KEY VOCABULARY FOR THE OLD AND NEW WORLDS COLLIDE

1. Bering Strait
2. Nomadic
3. Agriculture
4. Pueblo
5. Aztecs
6. Incas
7. Iroquois
8. Commodity
9. Kinship
10. Division of labor
11. Islam
12. Plantation
13. Songhai
14. Savanna
15. Benin
16. Kongo
17. Lineage
18. Prince Henry the Navigator
19. Hierarchy
20. Nuclear family
21. Renaissance
22. Reformation
23. Caravel
24. Dhow
25. Bartolomeu Diaz
26. Vasco da Gama
27. Christopher Columbus
28. Amerigo Vespucci
29. Taino
30. Hidalgos
31. Colonization
32. Triangular Trade
33. Middle Passage
34. Columbian Exchange
35. Treaty of Tordesillas
36. genocide

KEY VOCABULARY FOR THE EMERGENCE OF COLONIAL AMERICA

1. Hernando Cortes
2. Montezuma II
3. Tenochtitlan
4. Conquistadors
5. Francisco Pizarro
6. Incas
7. Aztecs
8. New Spain
9. Peninsulares
10. Mestizos
11. Encomienda
12. Juan Ponce de Leon
13. New Mexico
14. Pope's Rebellion
15. John Smith
16. Jamestown
17. Joint-stock company
18. Powhatan
19. The Virginia Company
20. Headright system
21. Indentured servants
22. Royal colony
23. Nathaniel Bacon
24. Puritans
25. John Winthrop
26. Separatists
27. Plymouth Colony
28. Massachusetts Bay Colony
29. Roger Williams
30. Anne Hutchinson
31. King Phillip's War
32. William Penn
33. New Netherland
34. Proprietor
35. Quakers

KEY VOCABULARY FOR THE COLONIES COMING OF AGE

1. Mercantilism
2. Parliament
3. Navigation acts
4. Dominion of New England
5. Glorious Revolution
6. Salutary neglect
7. King Charles II
8. Cash crop
9. Triangular trade
10. Middle passage
11. Olaudah Equiano
12. Stono Rebellion
13. The Enlightenment
14. Jonathan Edwards
15. Benjamin Franklin
16. The Great Awakening
17. Salem Witchcraft Trials
18. The French and Indian War
19. New France
20. George Washington
21. William Pitt
22. Pontiac
23. Proclamation of 1763
24. George Grenville
25. Sugar Act

KEY VOCABULARY FOR THE AMERICAN REVOLUTION

1. Stamp Act
2. Samuel Adams
3. Townshend Acts
4. Boston Massacre
5. Committees of correspondence
6. Boston Tea Party
7. King George III
8. Intolerable Acts
9. Martial law
10. Minutemen
11. Second Continental Congress
12. Olive Branch Petition
13. Common Sense
14. Thomas Jefferson
15. Declaration of Independence
16. Patriots
17. Loyalists
18. Battle of Bunker Hill
19. George Washington
20. Continental Army
21. Battle of Saratoga
22. Valley Forge
23. Trenton
24. Inflation
25. Profiteering
26. Friedrich von Steuben
27. Battle of Yorktown
28. General Charles Cornwallis
29. General Nathanael Greene
30. General Daniel Morgan
31. The Marquis de Lafayette
32. Egalitarianism
33. Treaty of Paris

KEY VOCABULARY FOR SHAPING A NEW NATION

1. REPUBLIC
2. REPUBLICANISM
3. Articles of Confederation
4. Land Ordinance of 1785
5. Northwest Ordinance of 1787
6. Shay's Rebellion
7. James Madison
8. Roger Sherman
9. Great Compromise
10. Three-Fifths Compromise
11. Federalism
12. Legislative branch
13. Executive branch
14. Judicial branch
15. Checks and balances
16. Electoral college
17. Ratification
18. Federalists
19. Antifederalists
20. The Federalist
21. Bill of Rights
22. Constitution

KEY VOCABULARY FOR LAUNCHING A NEW NATION

1. Judiciary Act of 1789
2. Alexander Hamilton
3. Cabinet
4. Bank of the United States
5. Democratic-Republicans
6. Two-party system
7. Protective tariff
8. Excise tax
9. Neutrality
10. Edmund Genet
11. Thomas Pinckney
12. Little Turtle
13. John Jay
14. Sectionalism
15. XYZ Affair
16. Alien and Sedition Acts
17. Nullification
18. Lewis and Clark
19. Aaron Burr
20. John Marshall
21. Judiciary Act of 1801
22. Midnight judges
23. Marbury vs. Madison
24. Judicial review
25. Louisiana Purchase
26. Sacajawea
27. Blockade
28. Impressment
29. Embargo
30. William Henry Harrison
31. Tecumseh
32. War hawk
33. Andrew Jackson
34. Treaty of Ghent
35. Armistice

KEY VOCABULARY FOR SECTIONALISM AND NATIONALISM

1. Eli Whitney
2. Interchangeable parts
3. Mass production
4. Industrial Revolution
5. Cotton gin
6. Henry Clay
7. American System
8. National Road
9. Erie Canal
10. Tariff of 1816
11. McCulloch vs. Maryland
12. John Quincy Adams
13. Nationalism
14. Adams-Otis Treaty
15. Monroe Doctrine
16. Missouri Compromise
17. Andrew Jackson
18. Democratic-Republican Party
19. Spoils system
20. Indian Removal Act
21. Trail of Tears
22. Daniel Webster
23. John C. Calhoun
24. Tariff of Abominations
25. Bank of the United States
26. Whig Party
27. Martin van Buren
28. Panic of 1837
29. William Henry Harrison
30. John Tyler

KEY VOCABULARY FOR REFORMING AMERICAN SOCIETY

1. Charles G. Finney
2. Second Great Awakening
3. Revival
4. Ralph Waldo Emerson
5. Transcendentalism
6. Henry David Thoreau
7. Civil disobedience
8. Utopian community
9. Dorothea Dix
10. Abolition
11. William Lloyd Garrison
12. Emancipation
13. David Walker
14. Frederick Douglass
15. Nat Turner
16. Antebellum
17. Gag rule
18. Elizabeth Cady Stanton
19. Lucretia Mott
20. Cult of domesticity
21. Sarah Grimke
22. Angelina Grimke
23. Temperance Movement
24. Seneca Falls Convention
25. Sojourner Truth
26. Cottage industry
27. Master
28. Journeyman
29. Apprentice
30. Strike
31. National Trades' Union

KEY VOCABULARY FOR WESTWARD HO!

1. Samuel F.B. Morse
2. Specialization
3. Market revolution
4. Capitalism
5. Entrepreneur
6. Telegraph
7. John Deere
8. Cyrus McCormick
9. Manifest Destiny
10. Treaty of Fort Laramie
11. Santa Fe Trail
12. Oregon Trail
13. Mormons
14. Joseph Smith
15. Brigham Young
16. "Fifty-Four Forty or Fight!"
17. Stephen F. Austin
18. Land grant
19. Antonio Lopez de Santa Anna
20. Texas Revolution
21. Alamo
22. Sam Houston
23. Republic of Texas
24. Annex
25. James K. Polk
26. Zachary Taylor
27. Stephen Kearny
28. Republic of California
29. Winfield Scott
30. Treaty of Guadalupe Hidalgo
31. Gadsden Purchase
32. Forty-niners
33. Gold rush

KEY VOCABULARY FOR THE UNION IN PERIL

1. Wilmot Proviso
2. Secession
3. Compromise of 1850
4. Popular sovereignty
5. Stephen A. Douglas
6. Millard Fillmore
7. Fugitive Slave Act
8. Personal liberty laws
9. Underground Railroad
10. Harriet Tubman
11. Uncle Tom's Cabin
12. Kansas-Nebraska Act
13. John Brown
14. Bleeding Kansas
15. Franklin Pierce
16. Nativism
17. Know-Nothing Party
18. Free-Soil Party
19. Republican Party
20. Horace Greeley
21. John C. Fremont
22. James Buchanan
23. Dred Scott
24. Roger B. Taney
25. Abraham Lincoln
26. Freeport Doctrine
27. Harpers Ferry
28. Confederacy
29. Jefferson Davis

KEY VOCABULARY FOR THE CIVIL WAR

1. Fort Sumter
2. Anaconda Plan
3. Bull Run
4. Stonewall Jackson
5. George McClellan
6. Ulysses S. Grant
7. Shiloh
8. David G. Farragut
9. Monitor
10. Merrimack
11. Robert E. Lee
12. Antietam
13. Emancipation Proclamation
14. Habeas corpus
15. Copperhead
16. Conscription
17. Fort Pillow
18. Income tax
19. Clara Barton
20. Andersonville
21. Gettysburg
22. Chancellorsville
23. Vicksburg
24. Gettysburg Address
25. William Tecumseh Sherman
26. Appomattox Courthouse
27. National Bank Act
28. Thirteenth Amendment
29. Red Cross
30. John Wilkes Booth

KEY VOCABULARY FOR RECONSTRUCTION

1. Andrew Johnson
2. Reconstruction
3. Radical Republicans
4. Thaddeus Stevens
5. Wade-Davis Bill
6. Freedman's Bureau
7. Black codes
8. Fourteenth Amendment
9. Impeach
10. Fifteenth Amendment
11. Scalawag
12. Carpetbagger
13. Hiram Revels
14. Sharecropping
15. Tenant farming
16. Ku Klux Klan (KKK)
17. Panic of 1873
18. Redemption
19. Rutherford B. Hayes
20. Samuel J. Tilden
21. Compromise of 1877
22. Home rule

KEY VOCABULARY FOR MIGRATION AND INDUSTRIALIZATION

1. Great Plains
2. Treaty of Fort Laramie
3. Sitting Bull
4. George A. Custer
5. Assimilation
6. Dawes Act
7. Battle of Wounded Knee
8. Longhorn
9. Chisholm Trail
10. Long drive
11. Homestead Act
12. Exoduster
13. Soddy
14. Morrill Act
15. Bonanza farm
16. Oliver Hudson Kelly
17. Grange
18. Farmers' Alliances
19. Populism
20. Bimetallism
21. Gold standard
22. William McKinley
23. William Jennings Bryan

KEY VOCABULARY FOR A SECOND INDUSTRIAL AGE

1. Edwin Drake
2. Bessemer Process
3. Thomas Alva Edison
4. Christopher Sholes
5. Alexander Graham Bell
6. Transcontinental railroad
7. George M. Pullman
8. Credit Mobilier
9. Munn vs. Illinois
10. Interstate Commerce Act
11. Andrew Carnegie
12. Vertical and horizontal integration
13. Social Darwinism
14. John D. Rockefeller
15. Sherman Antitrust Act
16. Samuel Gompers
17. American Federation of Labor (AFL)
18. Eugene V. Debs
19. Industrial Workers of the World (IWW)
20. Mary Harris Jones

KEY VOCABULARY FOR IMMIGRANTS AND URBANIZATION

1. Ellis Island
2. Angel Island
3. Melting pot
4. Nativism
5. Chinese Exclusion Act
6. Gentlemen's Agreement
7. Urbanization
8. Americanization Movement
9. Tenement
10. Mass transit
11. Social Gospel movement
12. Settlement houses
13. Jane Addams
14. Political machine
15. Graft
16. Boss Tweed
17. Patronage
18. Civil service
19. Rutherford B. Hayes
20. James A. Garfield
21. Chester A. Arthur
22. Pendleton Civil Service Act
23. Grover Cleveland
24. Benjamin Harrison

KEY VOCABULARY FOR LIFE IN THE NEW CENTURY

1. Louis Sullivan
2. Daniel Burnham
3. Frederick Law Olmsted
4. Orville and Wilbur Wright
5. George Eastman
6. Booker T. Washington
7. Tuskegee Normal and Industrial Institute
8. W.E.B. Du Bois
9. Niagara Movement
10. Ida B. Wells
11. Poll tax
12. Grandfather clause
13. Segregation
14. Jim Crow laws
15. Plessy vs. Ferguson
16. Debt peonage
17. Joseph Pulitzer
18. William Randolph Hearst
19. Ashcan School
20. Mark Twain
21. Rural free delivery (RFD)

KEY VOCABULARY FOR THE PROGRESSIVE ERA

1. Progressive movement
2. Florence Kelley
3. Prohibition
4. Muckraker
5. Scientific management
6. Robert M. LaFollette
7. Initiative referendum
8. Recall
9. Seventeenth Amendment
10. NACW
11. Suffrage
12. Susan B. Anthony
13. NAWSA
14. Upton Sinclair
15. The Jungle
16. Theodore Roosevelt
17. Square Deal
18. Meat Inspection Act
19. Pure Food and Drug Act
20. Conservation
21. NAACP
22. Gifford Pinchot
23. William Howard Taft
24. Payne-Aldrich Tariff
25. Bull Moose Party
26. Woodrow Wilson
27. Carrie Chapman Catt
28. Clayton Antitrust Act
29. Federal Trade Commission (FTC)
30. Federal Reserve System
31. Nineteenth Amendment

KEY VOCABULARY FOR AMERICAN IMPERIALISM

1. Queen Liliuokalani
2. Imperialism
3. Alfred T. Mahan
4. William Seward
5. Pearl Harbor
6. Sanford B. Dole
7. Jose Marti
8. Valeriano Weyler
9. Yellow journalism
10. U.S.S. Maine
11. George Dewey
12. Rough Riders
13. San Juan Hill
14. Treaty of Paris
15. Foraker Act
16. Platt Amendment
17. Protectorate
18. Emilio Aguinaldo
19. John Hay
20. Open Door notes
21. Boxer Rebellion
22. Panama Canal
23. Roosevelt Corollary
24. Dollar diplomacy
25. Francisco “Pancho” Villa
26. Emiliano Zapata
27. John J. Pershing

KEY VOCABULARY FOR THE FIRST WORLD WAR

1. Nationalism
2. Militarism
3. Allies
4. Central Powers
5. Archduke Franz Ferdinand
6. No man's land
7. Trench warfare
8. Lusitania
9. Zimmerman Note
10. Eddie Rickenbacker
11. Selective Service Act
12. Convoy system
13. American Expeditionary Force
14. General John J. Pershing
15. Alvin York
16. Conscientious objector
17. Armistice
18. War Industries Board
19. Bernard M. Baruch
20. Propaganda
21. George Creel
22. Espionage and Sedition Acts
23. Great Migration
24. Fourteen Points
25. League of Nations
26. Georges Clemenceau
27. David Lloyd George
28. Treaty of Versailles
29. Reparations
30. War-guilt clause
31. Henry Cabot Lodge

KEY VOCABULARY FOR THE INTERWAR YEARS

1. Nativism
2. Isolationism
3. Communism
4. Anarchists
5. Sacco and Venzetti
6. Quota system
7. John L. Lewis
8. Warren G. Harding
9. Charles Evans Hughes
10. Fordney-McCumber Tariff
11. Ohio gang
12. Teapot Dome scandal
13. Albert B. Fall
14. Calvin Coolidge
15. Urban sprawl
16. Installment plan
17. Prohibition
18. Speakeasy
19. Bootlegger
20. Fundamentalism
21. Clarence Darrow
22. Scopes Trial
23. Flapper
24. Double standard
25. Charles A. Lindbergh
26. George Gershwin
27. Georgia O'Keeffe
28. Sinclair Lewis
29. F. Scott Fitzgerald
30. Edna St. Vincent Millay
31. Ernest Hemingway
32. Zora Neale Hurston
33. James Weldon Johnson
34. Marcus Garvey
35. Harlem Renaissance

36. Claude McKay
37. Langston Hughes
38. Paul Robeson
39. Louis Armstrong
40. Duke Ellington
41. Bessie Smith

KEY VOCABULARY FOR THE GREAT DEPRESSION

1. Price support
2. Credit
3. Alfred E. Smith
4. Dow Jones Industrial Average
5. Speculation
6. Buying on margin
7. Black Tuesday
8. Great Depression
9. Hawley-Smoot Tariff Act
10. Shantytown
11. Soup kitchen
12. Bread line
13. Dust Bowl
14. Direct relief
15. Herbert Hoover
16. Boulder Dam
17. Federal Home Loan Bank Act
18. Reconstruction Finance Corporation
19. Bonus Army

KEY VOCABULARY FOR THE NEW DEAL

1. Franklin D. Roosevelt
2. New Deal
3. Glass-Steagall Act
4. Federal Securities Act
5. Agricultural Adjustment Act (AAA)
6. Civilian Conservation Corps (CCC)
7. National Industrial Recovery Act (NIRA)
8. Deficit spending
9. Huey Long
10. Eleanor Roosevelt
11. Works Progress Administration
12. National Youth Administration
13. Wagner Act
14. Social Security Act
15. Frances Perkins
16. Mary McLeod Bethune
17. John Collier
18. New Deal coalition
19. Congress of Industrial Organization (CIO)
20. *Gone With The Wind*
21. Orson Welles
22. Grant Wood
23. Richard Wright
24. *The Grapes of Wrath*
25. Federal Deposit Insurance Corporation (FDIC)
26. Securities and Exchange Commission (SEC)
27. National Labor Relations Board (NLRB)
28. Parity
29. Tennessee Valley Authority (TVA)

KEY VOCABULARY FOR THE SECOND WORLD WAR

1. Joseph Stalin
2. Totalitarian
3. Benito Mussolini
4. Fascism
5. Adolf Hitler
6. Nazism
7. Francisco Franco
8. Neutrality Acts
9. Neville Chamberlain
10. Winston Churchill
11. Appeasement
12. Nonaggression pact
13. Blitzkrieg
14. Charles de Gaulle
15. Holocaust
16. Kristallnacht
17. Genocide
18. Ghett
19. Concentration camp
20. Axis Powers
21. Lend-Lease Act
22. Atlantic Charter
23. Allies
24. Hideki Tojo
25. George Marshall
26. Women's Auxiliary Army Corps
27. A. Phillip Randolph
28. Manhattan Project
29. Office of Price Administration (OPA)
30. War Production Board (WPB)
31. Rationing
32. Dwight D. Eisenhower
33. D-Day
34. Omar Bradley
35. George Patton

36. Battle of the Bulge
37. V-E Day
38. Harry S. Truman
39. Douglas MacArthur
40. Chester Nimitz
41. Battle of Midway
42. Kamikaze
43. J. Robert Oppenheimer
44. Hiroshima
45. Nagasaki
46. Nuremberg trials
47. GI Bill of Rights
48. James Farmer
49. Congress of Racial Equality (CORE)
50. Internment
51. Japanese American Citizens League (JACL)

KEY VOCABULARY FOR THE COLD WAR

1. United Nations (UN)
2. Satellite nation containment
3. Iron curtain
4. Cold War
5. Truman Doctrine
6. Marshall Plan
7. Berlin airlift
8. North Atlantic Treaty Organization (NATO)
9. Chiang Kai-shek
10. Mao Zedong
11. Taiwan
12. 38th parallel
13. Korean War
14. HUAC
15. Hollywood Ten
16. Blacklist
17. Alger Hiss
18. Ethel and Julius Rosenberg
19. Joseph McCarthy
20. McCarthyism
21. H-bomb
22. Dwight D. Eisenhower
23. John Foster Dulles
24. Brinkmanship
25. Central Intelligence Agency (CIA)
26. Warsaw Pact
27. Eisenhower Doctrine
28. Nikita Khrushchev
29. Francis Gary Powers
30. U-2 incident
31. GI Bill of Rights
32. Suburb
33. Harry S. Truman
34. Dixiecrat
35. Fair Deal

36. Conglomerate
37. Franchise
38. Baby boom
39. Dr. Jonas Salk
40. Consumerism
41. Planned obsolescence
42. Mass media
43. Federal Communications Commission (FCC)
44. Beat movement
45. Rock'n' Roll
46. Jazz
47. Urban renewal
48. Bracero
49. Termination policy

KEY VOCABULARY FOR LIVING WITH GREAT TURMOIL, 1954-1975

1. John F. Kennedy
2. Flexible response
3. Fidel Castro
4. Berlin Wall
5. Hot line
6. Limited Test Ban Treaty
7. New Frontier
8. Mandate
9. Peace Corps
10. Alliance for Progress
11. Warren Commission
12. Lyndon Baines Johnson
13. Economic Opportunity Act
14. Great Society
15. Medicare and Medicaid
16. Immigration Act of 1965
17. Warren court
18. Reapportionment
19. Thurgood Marshall
20. Brown vs Board of Education
21. Rosa Parks
22. Martin Luther King, Jr.
23. Southern Christian Leadership Conference (SCLC)
24. Student Nonviolent Coordinating Committee (SNCC)
25. Sit-in
26. Freedom riders
27. James Meredith
28. Civil Rights Act of 1964
29. Freedom Summer
30. Fannie Lou Hamer
31. Voting Rights Act of 1965
32. De facto segregation
33. De jure segregation
34. Malcolm X
35. Nation of Islam
36. Stokely Carmichael

37. Black Power
38. Black Panthers
39. Kerner Commission
40. Civil Rights Act of 1968
41. Affirmative action
42. Ho Chi Minh
43. Vietminh
44. Domino theory
45. Dien Bien Phu
46. Geneva Accords
47. Ngo Dinh Diem
48. Vietcong
49. Ho Chi Minh Trail
50. Tonkin Gulf Resolution
51. Robert McNamara
52. Dean Rusk
53. William Westmoreland
54. Army of the Republic of Vietnam (ARVN)
55. Napalm
56. Agent Orange
57. Search-and-destroy mission
58. Credibility gap
59. Draft
60. New Left
61. Students for a Democratic Society (SDS)
62. Free Speech Movement
63. Dove
64. Hawk
65. Tet Offensive
66. Clark Clifford
67. Robert Kennedy
68. Eugene McCarthy
69. Hubert Humphrey
70. George Wallace
71. Richard Nixon
72. Henry Kissinger
73. Vietnamization
74. Silent majority
75. My Lai
76. Kent State University
77. Pentagon Papers

78. War Powers Act
79. Cesar Chavez
80. United Farm Workers Organizing Committee
81. La Raza Unida
82. American Indian Movement (AIM)
83. Betty Friedan
84. Feminism
85. National Organization for Women (NOW)
86. Gloria Steinem
87. Equal Rights Amendment (ERA)
88. Phyllis Schlafly
89. Counterculture
90. Haight-Ashbury
91. The Beatles
92. Woodstock

KEY VOCABULARY FOR PASSAGE TO A NEW CENTURY

1. Richard M. Nixon
2. New Federalism
3. Revenue sharing
4. Family Assistance Plan (FAP)
5. Southern strategy
6. Stagflation
7. OPEC (Organization of Petroleum Exporting Countries)
8. Realpolitik
9. Détente
10. SALT I Treaty
11. Impeachment
12. Watergate
13. H.R. Haldeman
14. John Ehrlichman
15. John Mitchell
16. Committee to reelect the President (CREEP)
17. John Sirica
18. Saturday Night Massacre
19. Gerald R. Ford
20. Jimmy Carter
21. National Energy Act
22. Human rights
23. Camp David Accords
24. Ayatollah Ruhollah Khomeini
25. Rachel Carson
26. Earth Day
27. Environmentalist
28. Environmental Protection Agency (EPA)
29. Three Mile Island
30. Entitlement program
31. New Right
32. Affirmative action
33. Reverse discrimination
34. Conservative coalition
35. Moral Majority

36. Ronald Reagan
37. Reaganomics
38. Supply-side economics
39. Strategic Defense Initiative
40. Sandra Day O'Connor
41. Deregulation
42. Environmental Protection Agency (EPA)
43. Geraldine Ferraro
44. George Bush
45. AIDS (acquired immune deficiency syndrome)
46. Pay equity
47. L. Douglas Wilder
48. Jesse Jackson
49. Lauro Cavazos
50. Antonia Coello Novello
51. Mikhail Gorbachev
52. Glasnost
53. Perestroika
54. INF Treaty
55. Tiananmen Square
56. Sandinistas
57. Contras
58. Operation Desert Storm

KEY VOCABULARY FOR THE U.S. IN TODAY'S WORLD

1. William Jefferson Clinton
2. H. Ross Perot
3. Hillary Rodham Clinton
4. NAFTA
5. Newt Gingrich
6. Contract with America
7. Al Gore
8. George W. Bush
9. Service sector
10. Downsize
11. Bill Gates
12. NASDAQ
13. Dotcom
14. General Agreement on Tariffs and Trade (GATT)
15. Information Superhighway
16. Internet
17. Telecommute
18. Telecommunications Act of 1996
19. Genetic engineering
20. Urban flight
21. Gentrification
22. Proposition 187
23. 911

www.ingramcontent.com/pod-product-compliance
Ingram Content Group UK Ltd.
Pitfield, Milton Keynes, MK11 3LW, UK
UKHW041901190726
13854UKWH00003B/1027

9 781312 108691